W9-BIY-128

AuthorHouse™
1663 Liberty Drive
Bloomington, IN 47403
www.authorhouse.com
Phone: 1-800-839-8640

© 2012 Pat. Moore. All Rights Reserved.
1993 Pat. Moore

No part of this book may be reproduced, stored in a retrieval system,
or transmitted by any means without the written permission of the author.

Published by AuthorHouse 02/02/12

ISBN: 978-1-4634-4583-6 (sc)

Printed in the United States of America

This book is printed on acid-free paper.

Because of the dynamic nature of the Internet, any web addresses or links contained in this book may have changed
since publication and may no longer be valid. The views expressed in this work are solely those of the author and do
not necessarily reflect the views of the publisher, and the publisher hereby disclaims any responsibility for them.

authorHOUSE®

Fall
Rain

By Pat. Moore

While walking on a pleasant fall day, my son Jonathan ran under a big oak tree that was shedding its brightly colored leaves. Playfully he exclaimed, "Look Mom it's raining!" It was to that innocent view I created this book.

ENJOY!

To
Tiffany,
Christopher,
and Jonathan

When it's winter,

Mom says . . .

"Bundle up.

It's cold."

When it's spring,

Mom says . . .

"Watch out for . . .
the puddles!"

When it's summer,

Mom says . . .

"Don't forget
your cap."

When it's fall,

Mom says . . .

"Enjoy!"

There is a time for everything,
and a season for every activity under heaven.

Ecc. 3:1

CPSIA information can be obtained
at www.ICGtesting.com
Printed in the USA
LVIC06n1940121214
418581LV00014B/71